REPAIR
YOUR LIFE
WORKBOOK

Supporting a Program for Recovery
from Incest & Childhood Sexual Abuse

Marjorie McKinnon

First Printing: June 2011
2nd Printing: January 2013

Learn more about the Lamplighters at www.TheLamplighters.org

ISBN-13: 978-1-61599-101-3

Published by
Loving Healing Press   www.LHPress.com
5145 Pontiac Trail   Tollfree 888-761-6268
Ann Arbor, MI 48105   Fax 734-663-6861

To request a free evaluation copy or purchase multiple copies for a non-profit or service agency at a special discount, please contact us through info@LHPress.com.

Distributed by Ingram Book Group (USA/CAN), Bertram's Books (UK)

The *REPAIR Your Life* Series is available in eBook editions for the Kindle, Nook, and Kobo eReaders

Contents

Introduction... i

A Program called R.E.P.A.I.R 1

Recognition 2
   Profile of a Childhood Sexual Abuse Victim 2

Entry 3
   The Twelve Steps 3

Process 5
   Construct a Magic Mirror 7
   Discovering Shame 14
   Family Tree Exercise 15

Awareness.. 20
   Influences...21
   Co-Dependency..24

Insight 26

Rhythm... 29

Resources for the Journey.. 34
   The Serenity Prayer..34
   The Optimist's Creed..34
   Support Groups 35

Introduction

Welcome to *REPAIR!* You have made a wise choice. If you work the REPAIR program with diligence and honesty you should be able to go from the dark side of life to the light side, the side that gives you wisdom, strength and peace. After working this program I went from being married to my third abuser, suicidal, in chronic despair and living part time in a women's shelter to being the happiest person I know. This program works!

The REPAIR program, an acronym, consists of six letters. Each letter and what it means is designed to prepare you for the next one. The Bridge of Recovery is a visual tool that helps you to feel centered as you work this program. You will feel yourself moving across that bridge and as you move you will feel stronger. You will begin to see the end of the bridge which means that all the "good stuff" is waiting for you. As you go from grief, painful flashbacks, severe depression, insomnia and all of the other qualities you will discover in the Profile of a Childhood Sexual Abuse Victim you will find yourself growing stronger, more in control of your own decisions, feeling emotions that had previously been rare in your life: joy, happiness, stability, wisdom. So much waits for you as you work this program.

You will begin by learning what each letter means in REPAIR and you will learn the Twelve Steps, another powerful tool available to you. You do not have to work it but it's there if you need some additional help. There are a host of Twelve Step programs for you to take advantage of while you are moving through REPAIR. I worked a Codependency program as well as an Incest Survivor Anonymous program. The important thing is that no matter which Twelve Step program you decide on, work the steps in the order in which they come. The first "R" in REPAIR means Recognition, admitting that you actually were a victim of child sexual abuse. The Profile of a Childhood Sexual Abuse Victim will help you with this. Once you get past that first tough one you decide what "E for entry" means. Decide what you want to do. Do you need a therapist to help you with this program? Do you need to work a Twelve Step as well or is the REPAIR program and a therapist enough. Should you try to find or start a Lamplighter Chapter? (www.thelamplighters.org) Some will find that all is needed is REPAIR.

This booklet gives you many treasures. Rules for a Good Sleep is only one of them. "P" is for Process and presents several exercises and ideas to help you heal. Reading books on recovery, listening to tapes, especially those of John Bradshaw, keeping a journal and talking into a tape recorder about your life, then listening to it back will all help enormously. The Bridge of Recovery begins your journey. You will take a sharp look at What waits behind you if you don't enter The Bridge, Fears you will encounter as you cross the bridge, and Solutions to combat them and finally, What lies on the other side of the bridge, waiting for you.

The first tool you will learn is how to construct a Magic Mirror and how to use it to your best advantage. It is a tool that is vital to this program. When you were a child living with abuse in your life you learned many Unhealthy Messages. You will think of Healthy Replacement Messages to counteract the damage done to you before you gather positive messages to put on your mirror. This booklet gives you many positive messages to get you started and you can add your own as time goes on. When I completed recovery, my large mirror was littered with messages, yellowed and curled, with only one small spot of the mirror for me to use. When guests asked me what that was on my mirror I would say, "Meet my new parents."

You will make a list of your shame as well as a list of things others have done to you that caused you shame. Then you will do the Family Tree Exercise. This puts the focus on those in your life that may have been perpetrators or enablers. Tips To Help You In the Midst of Your Journey is another valuable tool. You will need a rest and a few more ideas to help you.

The section on learning to create boundaries is extremely important. Most child sexual abuse victims haven't a clue on how to set a boundary. Give this section a lot of thought, perhaps ideas you would want to train your own child to use: don't talk to strangers (although 90% of child sexual abuse victims already know their perpetrator), learn to say NO (practice, practice, practice) – find a shirt that says, "What Part of No Don't You Understand" and wear it often, this is your body, you have a right to decide who can and cannot touch it, and most importantly, Tell, Tell, Tell. No matter what your perpetrator said about "don't tell", you know that silence is the single biggest reason why perpetrators don't get caught and stopped. Take your time, think of your own ways to create boundaries, write them down and little by little begin utilizing them.

Now you're ready for the [A]wareness. The Properties of Awareness are Sensibility, Prudence, Knowledge, Visualization, Feeling and Foresight. Write each down and understand what they mean, whether you had them in your life, and what kept you from having them. Next, comes the Family System Checklist and its own exercises: the Co-dependency Symptoms Checklist and Traits Before and After being molested,

[I]nsight is next. You are beginning to put the pieces of your puzzle together. Several exercises in this section of the workbook will guide you into discovering a vital fact in the healing process: "It was not your fault!"

Next we come to the fun part of the REPAIR Program, the final "R" which stands for Rhythm. When you were born you had your own natural rhythm, your own DNA so to speak. Once you were abused you lost that. In this program you are going to return to that natural rhythm you had in the beginning. More exercises await you to guide you into the discovery that the you that was born can and will return to that which you were meant to be. It is an exciting part of the program.

The workbook ends with a copy of The Serenity Prayer, (memorize and use it frequently), and the Optimist's Creed. By now you will be ready for both. It also includes a list of Support Groups and suggested websites. Take advantage of them for they contain much wisdom,

Best of luck. If you get stuck and need help, contact me at the Lamplighters website (Margie@thelamplighters.org).

Marjorie McKinnon

A Program called R.E.P.A.I.R

The *Bridge of Recovery* is a visual tool. The *Program* is a map to take you across that bridge.

The Stages

Recognition	Recognizing and accepting that your adult problems stem from childhood sexual abuse.
Entry	Entering a program of commitment to change your life for the better.
Process	Learning tools and techniques that will enable you to become healthy.
Awareness	The coming together of reality as you gather the pieces of the broken puzzle your life became, and begin assembling them to see the complete picture. Here you discover the properties of awareness that were God-given promises at birth, lost at the moment of sexual abuse.
Insight	Seeing the complete picture and beginning to return to what you were prior to being sexually violated.
Rhythm	Developing the natural rhythm you had before the incest happened, the blueprint that is the essence of your true nature, becoming who you really are.

Recognition

Abuse victims behave and respond in ways that are different from children raised in a emotionally healthy environment. In this book we will talk about two types of common denominations singular to children of childhood sexual abuse: individual and family systems. Family systems, which we will discuss later, show the type of forest you lived for now, let's concentrate on the individual ones, the trees.

These commonalities point to the origin of our unhappy lives. Once looked at, the picture becomes clearer. It is difficult to believe that a person who had a preponderance of these traits could live a happy life. Many of them, especially the individual traits, are common to anyone who suffered trauma in their childhood and never healed from the pain. This is a list of identification, not judgment. To help you with an honest appraisal, do the following exercise. Check any that apply to you.

Profile of a Childhood Sexual Abuse Victim

Individual behavior patterns	
People-pleasing and rescuing at an early age	
Insomnia	
Excessive need to control	
Obsessive, compulsive behavior patterns	
Needy	
Low self-esteem	
Suicidal	
Weak boundaries	
Unhealthy choices in members of the opposite sex	
Neurotic tendencies	
Addictions: drugs, alcohol, sex, food, relationships	
Eating disorders	
Chronic illness	
Manic-depressive behavior (bipolar)	
Severe depression	

Entry

There are three types of therapy we will discuss in this book: Individual, group therapy and programs and a combination of both.

Individual therapy requires enlisting the aid of a therapist. This sometimes begins at the urging of a family physician, a spiritual advisor, or a family member who can no longer bear to watch the individual suffer.

Group Therapy and Programs enlists the aid of Twelve Step Programs as well as incest recovery groups in local churches, domestic violence programs etc. The help that a Twelve Step program can give you is invaluable. For those not familiar with the Twelve Steps they are as follows:

The Twelve Steps

1. We admitted we were powerless over others and that our lives had become unmanageable.

2. We came to believe that a power greater than ourselves could restore us to sanity.

3. We made a decision to turn our lives over to the care of God as we understood God.

4. We made a fearless and searching moral inventory of ourselves.

5. We admitted to God, to ourselves, and to another human being the exact nature of our wrongs.

6. We were entirely ready to have God remove all these defects of character.

7. We humbly asked God to remove our shortcomings.

8. We made a list of people we had harmed and became willing to make amends to them all.

9. We made direct amends wherever possible, except when to do so would harm them or others.

10. We continued to take personal inventory and when we were wrong, promptly admitted it.

11. We sought through prayer and meditation to improve our conscious contact with God, praying only for knowledge of His will and the power to carry it out.

12. Having had a spiritual awakening as a result of these steps, we tried to carry this message to others and to practice these principles in all our affairs.

The third type of therapy would include a personal therapist and a program or support group. As you are preparing for your journey include a good night's sleep every night. Follow these rules for good sleep:

1. Keep caffeine intake to a minimum.

2. Use salt sparingly, if at all.

3. A hot bath with a good book, soft music, and a lighted candle (white for serenity) has a calming effect before bedtime.

4. Eat early in the evening and avoid large meals if possible.

5. Always retire at the same time.

6. Establish a comforting and stabilizing ritual prior to bedtime, i.e., lay out clothes for the next day, brush your teeth and bathe, set the clock, read something bland for a few minutes before turning the light out.

7. Avoid intense or worrisome phone calls before retiring, as well as any late-night dealings that may encourage stress (paying bills right before bedtime will usually ensure tossing and turning).

8. Don't exercise to excess in the evening—a short walk perhaps to ease tensions. Keep in mind that daily exercise improves sleep.

9. Make sure the room temperature is comfortable.

10. If you begin to toss and turn, get out of bed and fix a glass of warm milk or non-caffeine herbal tea. Insomnia intensifies once you begin worrying about it, so anything you can do to distract yourself eliminates the problem.

You are getting ready to cross the "Bridge of Recovery". This journey will take you from sorrow and anxiety to a place of joy.

Process

What Waits Behind Me If I Don't Enter The Bridge?

(Examples: shame, alcoholism, promiscuity, eating disorders, suicide, despair, health problems, unhappiness, poor choices, co-dependent behavior patterns, etc.).

Describe vividly each of these that are prevalent in your life as well as any others you can think of. (If you need more room use a separate sheet of paper.

_____

_____

_____

_____

Fears you will encounter as you cross the bridge, and solutions to combat them

(Examples: Problem—I'll feel too alone. Solution—I'll build a strong support group among friends, family and groups and utilize them whenever I feel this way. Problem—Looking at the pain of what happened is too overwhelming. Better the devil I know than the devil I don't. Solution—I'll check my list of all the things waiting for me at the end of the bridge, then compare it to the list behind me. My choice will be easier after that.) Write your own list and possible solutions

Problem	Solution

Keep in mind that inside each of us lies an untapped well of strength. We must be strong enough to cross the bridge; we have already survived so much.

What lies on the other side of the bridge, waiting for me?

(Examples: joy, strong self-esteem, healthy choices, honesty, peace, a feeling of being centered and capable, fulfillment, problem resolution oriented, serenity, etc.).

As you write, picture each of these to their fullest. They will act as a beacon guiding you across the bridge and one day will be a part of your life.

_____

_____

_____

_____

_____

Now, picture yourself entering the bridge. Like all journeys, you want this one to be successful. It is the most important one you will ever take. Crossing this bridge will bring you to a world beyond your wildest expectations. Reread the lists you have just written at least once a day to reinforce the purpose of your journey.

Construct a Magic Mirror

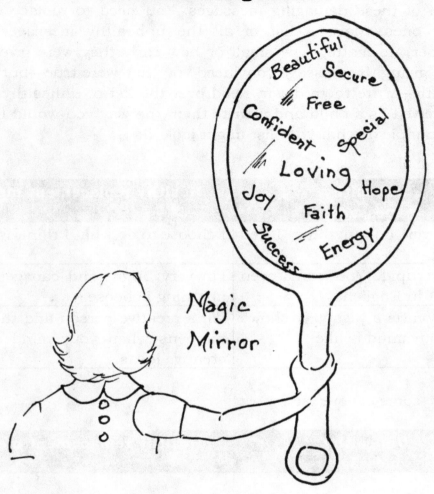

This may be the most significant thing you do as you cross that bridge. Your Magic Mirror will become your new parents. When you were a child, inevitably you received a lot of messages, some of which were unhealthy. *Don't touch yourself there. Bad girl. You're always lying about everything. I knew you were going to turn out like your father—no good. I'll tell you what you like and don't like. You're lazy.* And so on. Unfortunately, there were probably more negative messages than positive. Your brain is stuffed with them and what's worse, you no doubt believe them. It takes tremendous force for an adult to withstand these "not okay" messages, much less for a child.

You will need to get rid of every one. But it is not enough to rid yourself of these damaging messages. You need to replace them with healthy ones. Make a list of all the unhealthy messages you can remember, no matter how small or how early they were given. Even if the one giving the message convinced you they were true—but you know differently—write them down. Read over the list of unhealthy messages you received as a child and rewrite them the way you would like. Below is an example of what your list might look like.

Unhealthy message	Healthy replacement message
You never do anything I tell you.	I choose to do what I think is right.
You're stupid. You can't even get an A in English.	I'm very bright and can get an A in anything I choose.
Your room is a pigsty. It shows what your mind is like.	I'm a creative person and that's what happens when your mind is full of creative ideas.

Write some of your own.

Unhealthy message	Healthy replacement message

Next, you will need to gather affirmations for your Magic Mirror. Select any from the lists below that resonate with you. If you feel a strong emotional reaction to the affirmation, that is an indication you might have an issue around that. The following are some suggestions.

Healing

- No wound heals overnight, but little by little.
- As my heart heals, I will learn to love in exciting, powerful new ways.
- My maturity level will grow in proportion to the amount of pain I put behind me, and the wisdom I acquire as I move through the stages of REPAIR.

Courage

- The only antidote for fear is courage.
- I will trust that all is well, in spite of any fears I have.
- An unknown fear is better than a familiar pain.
- Whatever I fear grows in proportion to my obsession with it.
- I can get through dark situations. I only need to go as far as I can see. By the time I get there, I'll be able to see further.
- We all have monsters. Maybe it's fear of new situations. Maybe it's jealousy. The more attention I give the monsters, the more powerful they become.

Overcoming Problems

- A mistake is something I do; it's not who I am.
- There is no problem too difficult to handle with all the help available to me.
- All the problems are in my head. So are the solutions.
- Unfinished business doesn't go away.
- The only thing that's really the end of the world is the end of the world.

Anger

- I have a right to feel anger, and a responsibility to deal appropriately with my anger.
- I may need to get angry to set a limit, but I don't need to stay angry to enforce it.

Pain

- Recovery does not mean freedom from pain. Recovery means learning to take care of myself when I'm in pain.
- I can stop my pain and get control of my life.
- Pain is inevitable; suffering is optional. - Kathleen Casey
- I will accept pain and disappointment as part of life.
- If sorrow or pain enters my life, I can lean into it and become stronger.

Change

- I'm the only one who can change my life.
- The more choices I make, the more alive I feel. The more alive I feel, the healthier my choices.
- I am capable of making my most important decisions.
- Losing my freedom of choice is a bitter pill to swallow.
- There is no way to avoid changes in life, so why not make them positive ones?
- I will give up regrets about the past and fears about the future. I will make the most of this day.
- Healthy choices are all around. I can learn to make them.

Attitude

- "As we think, so we are." My mind works powerfully for my good, and just as powerfully to my detriment when I allow fear to intrude on my thoughts.
- A change of attitude is all I need to move from where I am to a better place.

- I need to believe that I deserve the best life has to offer. If I don't believe that, I need to change what I believe.
- If I always do what I've always done, I'll always get what I've always had.

Negativity

- I will avoid negative people.
- I can learn to let go of negative energy.
- If someone else has a bad day, it doesn't necessarily have anything to do with me.
- I don't have to believe lies.

Relationships

- I can recognize the difference between relationships that work and those that don't.
- Boundaries are worth every bit of time and energy it takes to set and enforce them. They will provide me with more time and energy.
- Friends are a joy. Today, I will reach out to my friends.
- If I think I'm the one who's finally going to change someone, I may be the one who gets victimized.
- My life will improve when I stop waiting for a rescuer, and begin to rescue myself.
- I can learn to act in the best interests of a relationship without neglecting my own best interests.
- I can own my own power wherever I am, wherever I go, whomever I'm with.
- I will surround myself with people who are learning to live and enjoy their own lives.
- I can take responsibility for myself. I don't have to take responsibility for other people.
- I need love, but I don't need destructive love.
- Controlling keeps me from enjoying other people, and it blocks their growth.

Self-esteem

- Being a victim is the path of least resistance.
- I can trust myself. I am wiser than I think.
- I will strive to be all that I can be.
- I'm the most important person in my universe.
- I can learn something worthwhile every day of my life.
- Life is not over till it's over.
- A strong person is not always big, but a big person is always strong.

Peace

- Walking on eggshells makes an irritating sound. I don't have to do it.
- Denial is when I pretend my circumstances are something other than what they are.
- I can learn to recognize when I'm reacting, rather than responding.
- When I've done all I can do, it's time to let go.
- When I'm feeling in chaos, I need to say and do as little as possible so I can restore my peace.
- I can ask for what I want and need. If I don't get it, I can figure out what to do next.
- Let go and let God.
- One day at a time.
- During stressful times, I can rely more heavily on my support system.
- Just for today, I will be strong enough to accept anything that comes my way.
- Today is the first day of the rest of my life.
- I will learn to use my head before I use my words.

***

Photocopy these suggestions or write each one on a piece of paper and tape them to your bathroom mirror. Hopefully you have a mirror large enough to hold all the wonderful new messages you will be taping over the next few months. Look through magazines, newspaper articles and one day at a time calendars. Listen to other people's wisdom and if something strikes you with a ring of healthy truth, write it down and put it on your mirror.

Read your messages every morning as you face yourself in the mirror. Little by little, you will be reprogramming yourself. Something magical happens with mirrors. It is as if you are literally taking these words of truth and planting them deep inside you. Like the childhood fairy tale: *Mirror, Mirror on the Wall, Who's the Fairest of Them all*, in time you will discover, *you are*. Treat these messages as valuable jewels, for the change they will bring has the highest value of anything you will ever acquire.

In times of stress, search your mirror for that particular truth that reflects the situation you are troubled about. As time goes on, you'll find that sooner or later everything you need to get well will show up on that mirror. Your unconscious mind will begin searching throughout your day for what you need. Eventually, you'll listen to what wise people say, and there, too, you will acquire words for your mirror, especially as you move across that bridge and begin spending time with healthy people.

Discovering Shame

Make a list of your shame, all those things you've done over the years that weigh heavily on your shoulders. Once you enter a Twelve Step Program, you will be doing this in more detail. Don't just list the things you did, list what others have done to you. This exercise is to get your feet wet and begin seeing the results of what happened to you when you were younger. Mostly, it is an attempt to see the truth. Armed with this, you can begin making quantum leaps in self-confidence.

Things I've done that caused shame.

_____

_____

_____

_____

_____

Things others have done to me that caused me shame.

_____

_____

_____

_____

_____

Family Tree Exercise

1. List all members of your nuclear (birth) family, starting with the oldest (parents) down to the youngest. Include yourself.

_____

_____

_____

_____

_____

_____

2. List mother's parents. _____

_____

3. List father's parents. _____

_____

4. List any aunts or uncles, grandfathers or grandmothers who lived with your birth family during your growing-up years.

_____

_____

5. List any known boundary violation behavior patterns that any family members may have exhibited, i.e., fondling inappropriate parts of your body, lewd suggestions and/or inappropriate remarks, etc. (no matter how minor) and who it was.

_____

_____

_____

6. List any comments you may have heard over the years regarding any of the above family members that would indicate they had boundary violation behavior patterns. Example: in my case, the well-known comment about my paternal grandfather was, "No woman is safe with him."

_____

_____

_____

_____

7. List any known sex offenders in the family, whether criminally prosecuted or not. If none, write "not applicable."

_____

_____

_____

8. Draw (using stick figures if necessary) the history of your family. Mark the members with inappropriate boundary violations with a red color. Mark yourself with a blue one. Draw a circle around the ones that could have protected you but didn't for whatever reason. Draw yourself in the middle and the others in varying degrees of closeness to you.

Tips to Help You in ihe Midst of Your Journey

Remember HALT: Hungry Angry Lonely Tired. Whenever you are having difficulty coping, remember to check this list. If any one of these is present, taking care of those needs will bring immediate emotional relief.

The Attitude of Gratitude—Daily list all your blessings in your mind. Everyone has some even though they may seem unimportant. Do you like to read? How about the movies? How about a special friend? Do you have lovely hands? A high energy level? Are you warm and affectionate? Do you like your job? If not, do you like your co-workers? Dig, dig, dig. You will find many more than you realized. Write them down. Something magical happens. Your blessings will begin to increase. And as they increase, so will your optimism about life and all its promises. These blessings will be an oasis in the midst of your journey across that bridge.

Create your own repertoire of "courage songs." Throughout the ages, people have adopted songs that gave them courage to keep living no matter how dark the times looked. Songs like *Ol' Man River, Deep River, Battle Hymn of the Republic, Swing Low Sweet Chariot, When you Walk Through A Storm, Amazing Grace,* and even our national anthem are courage songs. The songs are stirring, give us hope, and bind us to a promise. Find some of your own and whether you sing or not, use the words to give you courage. You will be surprised how much stronger you'll feel.

Listen to John Bradshaw's recordings—over and over.

Pamper yourself—by indulging in something that makes you feel good: an evening walk, lunch with a friend, buy flowers for no reason, schedule a massage therapy or spa visit, curl up with a good book, write a letter to someone you love telling them how well you are doing and all the new things you're learning.

Write a letter to your inner child—that small you who is waiting for the two of you to meet.

Take your life one day at a time, one hour at a time, and, if necessary, one minute at a time.

Call a supportive friend and share everything you're feeling.

Make a "wish list" of all you want to do with the rest of your life. Don't worry about whether it's realistic or not, just write it down. When you begin asking the universe for your dreams, it starts paying attention, for the world loves persistence and rewards those who practice it.

My Wish List!

_____

_____

_____

_____

_____

_____

_____

_____

_____

_____

_____

_____

Letting go of your anger is vital to the healing process. As you learn boundary setting, you will feel stronger. Feeling stronger alleviates some of the anger. Knowing that you cannot go back and change what happened but that you can go forward into a healing mode helps. Once you see the overall picture, especially the family history, it will be easier to approach this step.

Make a list of ways to create boundaries.

I will empower myself by:

_____

_____

_____

_____

_____

_____

_____

_____

_____

_____

Letting go of your anger is vital to the healing process. As you learn boundary setting, you will feel stronger. Feeling strong alleviates some of the anger. Knowing that you cannot go back and change what happened but that can go forward into a healing mode helps.

Awareness

Socrates, one of the world's greatest philosophers, once said, "An unexamined life is not worth living." Much truth lies in those words as well as much power. In this chapter you will need to draw on this to understand the importance of *Awareness*.

The quality of becoming aware includes many components. Sensibility, prudence, knowledge, visualization, feeling, and foresight are a few. They are siblings in the same family, gifts given to humans at birth. With these gifts, a human can be and do all to which they aspire. Let's take a closer look at these qualities before we proceed to see what part they played in our childhood sexual abuse issue.

Properties of Awareness

Sensibility	Visualization
Prudence	Feeling
Knowledge	Foresight

<u>Sensibility:</u> The capacity to reason, to use your head and think things through.

<u>Prudence:</u> uses that reason to discipline itself and once disciplined, life falls into order rather than chaos. One finds peace and tranquility in that order.

<u>Knowledge:</u> gathers experiences and sorts through them for the right answers. Knowledge is cognizant of the full range of truths available in ones own life.

<u>Visualization:</u> The ability to see all that you know, bringing it to life so that you can choose your next step. Create a vision, then step into it.

<u>Feeling:</u> The capacity to respond emotionally to everything that happens in our life. It is not feeling that get people in trouble; it is the actions they take based on those feelings.

<u>Foresight:</u> This simple act of looking forward takes us from the past to the present and into the future. We can do nothing about what has gone before but the present is in the arena of change. Healthy choices

made in the now will open a future that promises the fulfillment of your God-given potential.

Child sexual abuse has robbed us of these six God-given rights as well as many others. It is our hope that by the time you arrive at this part of REPAIR, you will begin to experience the joy that the components of Awareness brings.

Influences

Now it's time to take a look at the other influences on a child who has been sexually abused, the family systems ones. This is the forest that your trees (the individual aspects) grew under. In order to assemble the puzzle, check which of the following family systems fit into your picture.

Family System Checklist	
Patriarchal (or matriarchal) family system	
Obedient/co-dependent mother (father)	
Religiously regimented household	
Eldest daughter	
Alcoholic (or other addicted) parent: Mother [ ] Father [ ]	
Family history of sexual boundary violators	

Write a few words about how you think any checked item impacted your life while you were growing up. Was it positive or negative? In which way?

_____

_____

_____

_____

_____

_____

_____

_____

_____

_____

Write about how you think it changed your behavior as an adult.

_____

_____

_____

_____

_____

_____

_____

_____

_____

Were you the child of a patriarchal (or matriarchal) home? Did your patriarch abuse his responsibilities? List situations other than your sexual abuse where you were powerless as a child.

_____

_____

_____

_____

_____

_____

_____

_____

_____

_____

_____

_____

_____

Co-Dependency

Co-dependents have certain characteristics, some of which I mentioned earlier. The following is a checklist.

Co-dependency Symptoms Checklist	
They place other people's needs above their own.	
They are afraid to set and keep boundaries.	
They allow their mate to control them.	
They are afraid to ask for what they need.	
They are afraid to say what they're feeling.	
They are the giver in the relationship. This makes them angry.	
They are unhappy in the relationship and feel trapped.	
They hate the idea of solitude.	
They feel rejected if their mate spends time away from them.	
Unable to control their own pain, they try to control everyone around them.	

Did your mother or father have any traits from this list?

Write about how it felt to have a parent like this. Do *you* have any of the above traits?

_____

_____

_____

_____

_____

_____

It's a proven fact that *Child molesters pick the most obedient child in the school yard.* As you progress further into recovery, you'll begin to understand this. You see yourself as that pawn in a game of chess, realizing you could not have changed your family history or the part you played in it.

List traits and behavior patterns you had prior to being molested, then list those you had as a result of being molested.

Traits before being molested	Traits after being molested

Insight

One of the ways in which he accomplished this purpose was through the use of subliminal messages. Subliminal messages have diabolical power and take root even more than blatant ones. If your perpetrator was your father, his subliminal message could have been, *It's okay to have sex with married men.* This may have been one of the directions you followed as an adult, thereby breeding self-loathing. It is difficult to have healthy self-esteem when you feel you are covered with garbage. Another message may have been, *It's not okay to set sexual boundaries.* What subliminal messages planted themselves in your unconscious, paving the way for unhealthy behavior?

Subliminal Messages	Behaviors I Adopted As A Result

The insight acquired by working this program will prompt you to establish a whole new belief system—your own. Along with that, you'll seek out mature behavior patterns. Test your own ability to recognize new-found maturity. Some examples are: I will not judge until I have all the evidence; When I am wrong, I will apologize; My behavior will be gracious even toward those I dislike; I will remember that life is too short to be little, etc. List some of your own and those you would like to adopt.

Mature Behavior Patterns

Make a list of those qualities that you think are the "real love" attributes you would like to have received from your parents. Examples might be: They not only listen to what we have to say, but they hear us; they encourage us to be all that we can be; they tell us verbally and physically (with appropriate affection) that they care and are happy we are in their life. What qualities did you not get from your parents that are "real love" qualities?

"Real Love" Qualities	Did I Receive or Not?

In the realization of this truth, we discover we have never validated these qualities. Make a list. Leave nothing out. Realize that some of these are not new, but have been a part of us for most of our lives. As an example: perhaps when you were a child you were caring and sensitive to the needs of others. That may be why your particular sexual abuse was more painful to you than to a less sensitive person. Now you can view that quality as a great gift that you have to give others.

My Wonderful Qualities	How Long Have I Had Them?

Take a look at your list. Remind yourself that this is a part to the complete picture that you never saw. You realize you have value. You are a whole person. You have choices. Saying no is easier. Courage develops. With it comes a healthier ego, stronger self-esteem, and wise decisions. You are approaching the end of the bridge. Can you feel the lightening of your heart?

Now, it's time to rid ourselves of our shame. Find a place of peace and strength. Picture all of your shame, all the negativity you carried for so long. Symbolically place it in a large gunny sack and throw it away. Heave it into the universe once and for all. It was never yours to begin with. All you have done is carry it or others who should have been carrying it themselves.

Rhythm

The path we took in life and the decisions we made at the crossroads were shaped by our experiences. As a child of sexual abuse, those experiences were a horror most people cannot imagine. Nor would they want to. People who were free to become all they wanted to be cannot know what it is like to live in a prison. In completing this program you are releasing yourself from that prison.

Once you are free, you begin to return to one of the greatest joys all living creatures have—their own rhythm. Even animals have their own rhythm and would fight mightily against anyone who tried to take it away. If you go back far enough, you can remember waking at the same time every morning and getting tired at the same time every night. You had a time for hunger, a time for energy, and a time for languor. Being a part of that natural rhythm brought joy as well as serenity. Life, predictable and comfortable, contained meaning and purpose. It was like a dance, one where we moved freely through our own universe, bending and swaying our bodies in time to our inner voices. You are now ready to return to your own rhythm.

Do the following exercise to return to what you really are. Describe your natural rhythm in the following areas:

(i.e., I sleep deep or light, I snore, I hug pillows, I'm a fast talker, rowdy humor etc.)

Sleeping _____

_____

_____

Conversation _____

_____

_____

Humor _____

_____

_____

Hobbies and interests _____

_____

_____

_____

My favorite people would look like:_____

_____

_____

My favorite foods are: _____

_____

_____

_____

My value system includes: _____

_____

_____

_____

My political affiliation and beliefs are: _____

_____

_____

_____

My religious and spiritual beliefs and needs are: _____

_____

_____

_____

    List other areas of your life, your likes and dislikes. Show a clear picture of everything you are the most comfortable with. How many are in your life now? Why are the others not?

    The more we choose to follow the path of our own nature, the happier we'll be. As always, this guideline must be tempered with wisdom. The ability to use common sense as a tool to navigate through life is invaluable. Unfortunately, the only thing wrong is that it isn't very common, one of the reasons the world is in such a tangle. Some of the basic rules are:

1. Do whatever works.
2. If it's not broken, don't fix it.
3. Let sleeping dogs lie.
4. Respond, don't react.
5. Choose your battles wisely.
6. Use your head before using your words.

    How many others can you think of? Keep in mind that using common sense as well as staying within your own rhythm brings stability and serenity.

Take a look at all aspects of your life. Then write down whether or not you are satisfied with them. If not, write down possible changes you could make. Use the following exercise as a guideline:

Personal relationships: ____Satisfied ____Not Satisfied

What I can do to change it?_____

_____

Career Choice: ____Satisfied ____Not Satisfied

What I can do to change it?_____

_____

Residence: ____Satisfied ____Not Satisfied

What I can do to change it?_____

_____

Hobbies and Interests: ____Satisfied ____Not Satisfied

What I can do to change them?_____

_____

List other aspects of your life and ways to change them.

_____

_____

_____

_____

_____

Now make the following lists:

Things I always wished I could do but never did:

_____

_____

_____

_____

Ways I can accomplish each one of them:

_____

_____

_____

_____

Your world is unlikely to be perfect after recovery. Life goes on and sometimes it contains heartache and challenges. There will be deaths and financial stress; you may not find the man/woman of your dreams, and so on. But in your pre-recovery days when these things happened, it felt like the end of the world. Now you know it never was. Now you're better equipped to take things in stride

Resources for the Journey

The Serenity Prayer

God, grant me the serenity

to accept the things

I cannot change,

the courage

to change the things I can,

and the wisdom to know

the difference.

The Optimist's Creed

I Promise:

To be so strong that nothing can disturb my peace of mind.

To talk health, happiness and prosperity to every person I meet.

To make all my friends feel there is something special in them.

To look at the sunny side of everything and make my optimism come true.

To think only of the best, to work only for the best, and expect only the best.

To be just as enthusiastic about the success of others as I am about my own.

To forget the mistakes of the past and press on to the greater achievement of the future.

To wear a cheerful countenance at all times and give every living creature I meet a smile.

To give so much time to the improvement of myself that I have no time to criticize or judge others.

To be too large for worry, too noble for anger, too strong for fear and too happy to permit the presence of trouble.

From *Your Forces and How to Use Them* by Christian D. Larson (1912).

Support Groups

Twelve Step Programs

For the phone number of a Twelve Step Program your area of the USA, call 1-800-555-1212, and ask for the Program of your choice below and the phone number of the nearest branch location.

- Alcoholics Anonymous
- Al-anon
- Co-Dependents Anonymous
- Overeaters Anonymous
- Narcotics Anonymous

Suggested Websites

www.catharsisfoundation.org Catharsis Foundation is a non-profit incorporated in Calgary Alberta in 2004 for survivors of ALL forms of child abuse—internationally

www.thelamplighters.org The Lamplighters is a movement founded by Marjorie McKinnon, author of *REPAIR Your Life*, for survivors of incest and child sexual abuse. Emphasizes the importance of REPAIRing the damage done and recommends using the program REPAIR as a model for recovery.

www.angelashelton.com Angela Shelton is a public speaker, author, actress, writer and advocate for victims of child sexual abuse.

www.mskinnermusic.com Mike Skinner offers Hope, Healing & Help for Trauma, Abuse & Mental Health through music, resources and advocacy

www.familywatchdog.us A website that lists names and addresses of all known sex offenders in the US.

www.preventchildabuse.org Since 1972, *Prevent Child Abuse America* has led the way in building awareness, providing education and inspiring hope to everyone involved in the effort to prevent the abuse and neglect of our nation's children.

www.rainn.org *The Rape, Abuse & Incest National Network* is the nation's largest anti-sexual assault organization and has been ranked as one of "America's 100 Best Charities" by *Worth* magazine.

www.recoverybooks.com The recovery and self-help bookstore.

www.prevent-abuse-now.com This website, also called *Pandora's Box* offers information, offenses, prevention and protection regarding child sexual abuse.

www.acestudy.org The *Adverse Childhood Experiences Study* is an ongoing collaboration between the Centers for Disease Control and Prevention and Kaiser Permanente. It is perhaps the largest scientific research study of its kind, analyzing the relationship between multiple categories of childhood trauma (ACEs), and health and behavioral outcomes later in life.

www.stopcsa.org The goal of *Stop The Silence* is to stop child sexual abuse and related forms of violence by changing societal relationships among and between groups.

www.childmolestationprevention.org *The Child Molestation Research & Prevention Institute* is a national science-based nonprofit organization dedicated to preventing child sexual abuse through research, education, and family support.

www.darkness2light.org *Darkness to Light* is a national nonprofit organization and initiative that seeks to diminish the incidence and impact of child sexual abuse, so that more children will grow up healthy and whole.

REPAIR for Children (6-12)

If you know of any child between the ages of 6 and 12 that needs to recover from child sexual abuse please get REPAIR For Kids by Marjorie McKinnon, also published by Loving Healing Press

Acclaim for REPAIR For Kids:

"The author has set up a six-stage program which she identifies this way: Recognition, Entry, Process, Awareness, Insights and Rhythm. There are worksheets for the child to use in learning about their feelings, building self-esteem and optimism, learning the difference between healthy and unhealthy messages, learning skills to soothe the inner-child, how to reveal inner feelings through drawing, breaking free from false shame, cultivating self-care skills and practices, learning about boundaries and bodies, and how to return to the natural rhythm and flow of life.

The author has used simple terms and created easy tools to help any child work through the devastation of sexual abuse. Highly recommended".

—F. M. Meredith, author
Kindred Spirits and *No Sanctuary*

"*REPAIR for Kids* provides a comprehensive, honest and passionate approach for children recovering from sexual abuse. Children will benefit from this book, and be encouraged to continue on their recovery journey."

—Jill Osborne, Ed.S, author
Sam Feels Better Now

Learn more about this revolutionary system at **www.TheLamplighters.org**

Just released! REPAIR for TEENS

9 781615 991013